Praise for *The l*

In less than the time it takes to read an hour-long script, Kat Montagu will show you, in an entertaining manner, how to master script and screenplay formatting. How do you suggest a new shot without annoying the director? What's the difference between ellipses and a double dash in dialogue? How have parentheticals evolved? When and how often do you use them? What do CAPITALIZED WORDS mean in an action line? How do you make actors emphasize the words you want them to emphasize? (Spoiler alert — the answer has nothing to do with italics.) Most importantly, there's a sexy ghost!

HART HANSON (*Bones*)

This genius learn-as-you-laugh guide teaches you script formatting in a way that's pain-free, memorable, and logical. In my nearly 30-year career, I have had to learn formatting on the street, copying the examples I happened to come across, and this would've been a great help to me. In fact, even now, reading it makes certain things clear that I've never fully understood. I highly recommend this book!

JANE ESPENSON (*Buffy the Vampire Slayer, Battlestar Galactica*)

Kat Montagu has made the absolutely essential craft of formatting scripts correctly a joy to know: *The Dreaded Curse* is clear, concise, AND entertaining. Comprehensive and easy to use, I've recommended the original edition to countless students, teachers, film story editors, and to my fellow writing mentors. This expanded edition is now a Must-Have for scripted showrunners in Comedy or Drama, TV staffers, and script coordinators, too. Think of it as a silver bullet for every time-sucking format debate and unnecessary format corrections from your teams, as well as a trustworthy style guide when working with material outside your usual expertise. An excellent tool.

KAREN WALTON (*Ginger Snaps, Queer as Folk, Orphan Black*)

Kat has crafted an elegant way to make the importance of screenplay formatting not only informative but also entertaining. A must-have resource for all new screenwriters.

SIMON BARRY (*Continuum, Warrior Nun*)

Kat Montagu's primer on scriptwriting format is a lot of fun, extremely useful, and quite indispensable. Not only is reading this book a refresher course for any seasoned writer, but I learned a few things I'd always wondered about, like when to use ellipses versus double dashes and how to maximize the impact of an action sequence on the page. With formatting instructions cleverly written into a charming narrative, this ingenious guide should be a must-have for every student entering film school.

MARIA JACQUEMETTON (*Mad Men, The Romanoffs*)

THE DREADED CURSE

SCREENPLAY FORMATTING

FOR FILM & TELEVISION

THE DREADED CURSE

SCREENPLAY FORMATTING
FOR FILM & TELEVISION

KAT MONTAGU

THREE OCEAN PRESS

Library and Archives Canada Cataloguing in Publication

Title: The dreaded curse : screenplay formatting for film & television / Kat Montagu.
Other titles: Dreaded curse of screenplay formatting | Screenplay formatting for film & television
Names: Montagu, Kat, 1967- author.
Description: Originally published under title: The dreaded curse of screenplay formatting. 2019.
Identifiers: Canadiana (print) 20200390937 | Canadiana (ebook) 20200391194 | ISBN 9781988915333 (softcover) | ISBN 9781988915340 (EPUB)
Subjects: LCSH: Motion picture authorship. | LCSH: Television authorship.
Classification: LCC PN1996 .M66 2021 | DDC 808.2/3—dc23

Editor: Kyle Hawke
Copyeditor: SJ Trowhimchuk
Proofreader: Kyle Hawke
Book Designer: PJ Perdue
Cover Designer: Elizabeth Mackey
Author Photo: Dirk Erkau

Three Ocean Press
8168 Riel Place
Vancouver, BC, V5S 4B3
778.321.0636
info@threeoceanpress.com
www.threeoceanpress.com

First publication, December 2020

To Rob and Lydia

Acknowledgements

Thanks to Greg Beal for his inspiring 1996 format guide, *For a Few Days More.*

Many thanks to my many students over the years for table reading this guide in my class.

Thanks to my boss, Michael Baser, for being so gracious, funny, and kind.

Thanks to Dirk Erkau for his flattering photography.

Kudos to Elizabeth Mackey for the awesome cover.

Kudos to SJ Trowhimchuk for the copy and format editing. All subsequent errors are my own.

Kudos to PJ Perdue for the wonderful book design.

Kudos to Three Ocean Press's Kyle Hawke for encouraging me to expand this, for wanting to publish it, and for his eagle eye.

Contents

Introduction

A screenwriter and story editor herself, Kat needed a simple up-to-date format guide in the Hollywood style, so she wrote this one. After many requests from students and former students that she publish this guide, here it is.

Kat designed *The Dreaded Curse* to be fun to read, but more importantly to contain every element you might need to format your modern feature film screenplay or TV pilot script correctly.

Formatting styles do change over time, so read recent scripts and keep your eyes open for new editions.

FEATURE-LENGTH FILM

THE DREADED CURSE
SCREENPLAY FORMATTING
FEATURE-LENGTH FILM

by

Kat Montagu

First Draft

(Any draft that no one has
optioned yet is a FIRST DRAFT,
no matter how many versions
you've written)

Based on...
(Source material and author)

(The producer needs to acquire
the rights and you shouldn't
infringe on someone else's
copyright or commit plagiarism)

Inspired by
For a Few Days More
by
Greg Beal
1996

yourname@youremail.com

FADE IN:

INT. HAUNTED MANOR HOUSE DINING ROOM - NIGHT

An old-fashioned, dark red dining room features a large oak table, carved chairs, candles, and mirrors.

HAZEL (24), an intense witch in a black dress, and ROSETTA (22), her cute hipster sister, CLINK their wine glasses and drink.

Before them sits a beautiful meal, perfectly cooked.

Hazel pours herself another glass of wine.

> HAZEL
> Could you tell me what you've
> learned at film school about
> formatting screenplays? I have
> a great idea for a horror film.

> ROSETTA
> Is it about witches?

> HAZEL
> No way. No one believes in
> witches and vampires are over.
> No. It's called Zombie Romance.

> ROSETTA
> Okay, some stuff I remember:
> Screenplays are always in
> present tense. The first time
> you introduce a character in
> description, you CAPITALIZE the
> name, indicate the age, and give
> a very brief description.

Rosetta serves the food.

Hazel takes a large gulp of her wine.

> HAZEL
> What about fonts?

                    ROSETTA
          Screenplay font should look like
          typewriter font, so Courier 12.
                    (scrolls though her
                    phone)
          I have an awesome handout. I think
          I emailed it to myself:

Rosetta shows Hazel an email from rosetta@witch.cov.
No subject line, simple text: Formatting Handout.

                    ROSETTA
          Oh. There's no attachment.

                    HAZEL
                    (pulls out a wand)
          Don't worry. I'll put a spell on
          you to remember it in detail and
          tell it to me.
                    (waves her wand)
          Remember, remember, the 5th of
          November.

Hazel hits Rosetta with her wand. There is a flash of
light and a BANG. A puff of smoke lingers.

                    HAZEL (CONT'D)
          Okay. Margins?

                    ROSETTA
          Around 1.5 inches or 3.8 cm.

Hazel hears CREAKING NOISES and lifts her head.

                    HAZEL
          When someone's about to speak?

                    ROSETTA
          Put the character's name about
          3.5 inches or 9 cm from the left
          margin, in caps.

                    HAZEL
          Dialogue margins?

ROSETTA
2.5 inches or 6.3 cm on each side,
leaving 3.5 inches or 9 cm for
each line of dialogue. You could
set Word up to do all of this
using Format - Style — New, but
screenwriting software does it
so much better.

HAZEL
What if there's a page break?

ROSETTA
You can split long chunks of
dialogue across a page break.
To add a page break in the middle
of a chunk of dialogue, add
(MORE) centered at the bottom,
to show that the dialogue will
continue, then (CONT'D) next
to the character name to show
that the dialogue started on
the page before. No need for
CONTINUED at the top and bottom
of every page.

HAZEL
And what about action-description
paragraphs?

ROSETTA
Keep each scene heading with at
least one line of action that
follows. Screenwriting software
protects against "widows and
orphans" so screenplays never
have characters separated from
their dialogue or scene headings
separated from their action.

HAZEL
Can I use bold or italics for
emphasis?

                    ROSETTA
        No.

A loud CREAK comes from the hallway.

Hazel grabs her phone, jumps up, and opens the door.

Rosetta looks mournfully at her meal, then follows her.

The door SLAMS shut behind Rosetta.

INT. HAUNTED MANOR HOUSE HALLWAY - NIGHT

Hazel glances up and down the hallway. A loud THUNK
comes from the dining room they just left.

                    HAZEL
                (scared)
        Yeah, yeah. This Ghost has been
        bothering me ever since--

A BANG interrupts Hazel.

                    HAZEL (CONT'D)
        That's why I invited...

Hazel trails off, listening.

                    ROSETTA
        Notice the double dash-- shows an
        interruption and the ellipsis...
        show a character choosing to stop
        talking mid-sentence.

          HAZEL   ROSETTA
That's good to know. What   Grab the dialogue
happens if both of us   couplet, and click
talk at the same time or   Format — Dual Dialogue.
if our dialogue overlaps?   In Word, use Format -
                              Columns.

Another CREAK and a HOWL from the dining room.
Hazel SCREAMS and races for the exit.

ROSETTA (CONT'D)
CAPITALIZE all sounds in your
action paragraphs. Don't panic.
I'm sure it's just your cat.

Rosetta tries to follow her outside.

Something invisible stops her at the doorway.

Her smile vanishes.

INT./EXT. HAUNTED MANOR HOUSE - NIGHT

Rosetta BANGS her fists against the invisible barrier.

Hazel sees Rosetta struggling at the door.

Rosetta pulls her wand out of her left boot.

HAZEL
(calling)
Look at the last scene heading --
otherwise known as a slug line --
above you.
(beat)
Scene headings are always CAPPED,
like this: INT. or EXT. then a
location, then space, dash,
space, then DAY or NIGHT.
Recently, some Hollywood
screenwriters have also started
bolding their scene headings.
(beat)
Occasionally people use INT./EXT.
for a back-and-forth scene, but
only if there must be one camera
inside and one outside with back-
and-forth shots.

Rosetta points her wand at the door.

Hazel sees sparks FIZZLE around the doorframe.

EXT. HAUNTED MANOR HOUSE - NIGHT

Rosetta bursts through the door, PANTING. She returns her wand to her left boot.

Hazel hugs her.

                    HAZEL
          You made it!

Fog starts to drift towards them from the open doorway. It seems ominous.

                    HAZEL (CONT'D)
          Fog, like snow or rain or raining
          frogs, is a practical effect
          (sometimes written as SFX for
          Special Effects). Anything
          computer-generated is VFX or CGI,
          but, as always, write what you
          want to see on screen then start
          a new paragraph when you imagine
          a new shot.
               (beat)
          I'm scared.

                    ROSETTA
          I could tell you about
          parentheticals?

                    HAZEL
               (sarcastically)
          Oh joy.

Hazel pulls Rosetta towards her green VW Beetle.

Rosetta rushes around to the passenger side.

Hazel presses the button on the fob. BEEP.

Rosetta gets in.

                    ROSETTA
          For decades, writers told actors
          how to say their lines using
          parentheticals.
                    (quietly, sadly,
                    angrily)
          Now that's only necessary if it's
          not obvious.
                    (sarcastically or
                    ironically)
          Now writers use them most often
          for brief actions by the
          character who is talking.

                    HAZEL
          Can you just shut up about
          screenplay formatting now,
          please?

                    ROSETTA
          Not until I finish. You cast a
          spell on me to remember,
          remember?

                    HAZEL
          Oh god. Really?

                    ROSETTA
          Really. Parentheticals belong
          between the character's name and
          their dialogue, indented about
          half an inch more than the
          dialogue. With most screenwriting
          software, write the character
          name, then hit Enter, then Tab.

The fog starts to take the shape of a figure. Scary.

                    ROSETTA (CONT'D)
          Just don't overdo it. No more
          than one or two parentheticals
          per page.

Both sisters strap on seat belts. Hazel STARTS the
engine.

The VW Beetle ROARS down the driveway.

EXT. HIGHWAY - NIGHT

On the highway, the VW Beetle merges with existing
traffic. They veer across into oncoming traffic.

A black van is headed straight for them. The van is
boxed in by two other vehicles.

The VW Beetle seems doomed.

PRE-LAP: HEARTBEAT speeds up.

> ROSETTA (PRE-LAP) (V.O.)
> Watch out!

INT. VW BEETLE - NIGHT

Rosetta clutches the dash.

Hazel spots an opening and drives back onto the correct
side of the road.

> ROSETTA (CONT'D)
> A pre-lap like that gives a
> snippet of sound or dialogue from
> the next scene.
> (beat)
> Feature film writers rarely use
> CUT TO: between scenes anymore,
> because a new scene heading
> implies a cut. But some writers
> use DISSOLVE TO: on the righthand
> margin, between two scenes which
> take place in the same location,
> to indicate the passage of time.

Hazel stares into the rearview mirror.

Rosetta peers around to look.

The ominous fog is still following them. A car drives
right through it. BEEPING its horn.

                    HAZEL
          Could it be--

                    ROSETTA
          Take the next left. We don't want
          to describe the entire journey in
          real time, so let me show you how
          to write a montage.

EXT. COUNTRY ROADS - NIGHT

MONTAGE:

- The VW Beetle jumps a small bridge.

- The VW Beetle swerves around a tight corner.

- The VW Beetle floats across a small river.

- The VW Beetle travels past a pub, leaking water.

- The VW Beetle passes a sign. "Abandoned Air Field."

END MONTAGE

                    ROSETTA (V.O.)
          A montage is linked by theme. "A
          couple falls in love" or "A boxer
          gets back into shape." You can
          even use stock footage. A chase
          scene with no dialogue could be a
          good montage. So could a series
          of juxtaposed actions over a
          month.

EXT. AIRFIELD — DAY

FAST ENERGETIC MUSIC begins.

This is an old airfield, once perhaps used by the
military, but covered with grass and moss now.

There are no lights in the tower.

The VW Beetle swerves all over the place, trying to lose the patch of fog that follows.

SERIES OF SHOTS:

- The VW Beetle comes to a halt.

- Rosetta pulls out two brooms.

- Hazel puts on lipgloss.

- Rosetta pulls a pair of goggles down.

- Hazel and Rosetta stand astride their brooms.

END SERIES OF SHOTS

          ROSETTA (V.O.)
    In contrast, a series of shots
    takes place in the same place,
    over a short period -- one
    evening, perhaps -- but lets you
    link shots to abbreviate that
    time. So the highlights of a
    game, a school prom, or a fight
    scene.

EXT. 500 FEET UP - NIGHT

Hazel and Rosetta fly on broomsticks.

Behind them, unseen, a cloud in the shape of a man shadows them.

          HAZEL
    Some birthday this is.

          ROSETTA
    For the audience to see the date,
    it needs to look like this:

SUPER:
January 23, YEAR

                    ROSETTA (CONT'D)
          Still, we got away from that
          Ghost at last. He won't look for
          us here.

Hazel glances back and sees the Ghost flying behind
them.

                    HAZEL
          Oh my god. There he is. Look.
          Let's lose him in that cloud
          cover.

                    ROSETTA
          Okay. Check out this action
          scene.

EXT. CLOUDS — NIGHT

Rosetta and Hazel race alongside a stormcloud.

SUDDENLY,

the Ghost whips around the corner of a nearby cloud --

— racing quickly towards them.

Rosetta speeds up and —

— loops the loop —

Hazel plunges downward —

— into a small fluffy white cloud.

The Ghost can't decide — he hesitates — the storm
cloud overtakes him and everything goes dark.

THUNDER CLAPS

Then lightning strikes -- Hazel and Rosetta double back
together again and look for —

— the Ghost —

—— The Ghost emerges from the storm cloud just as THUNDER CLAPS ——

—— and lightning strikes him.

Rather than damaging him, the lightning makes ——

THE GHOST (26) more visible, a real person now, and surprisingly handsome.

Hazel sees this and hesitates ——

—— slowing down on her broom.

Rosetta looks back to see what's keeping Hazel.

The additional weight of a corporeal body weighs down the Ghost. He starts to sink, and looks scared.

Hazel flies below him and lets him land safely on the back of her broomstick.

He clutches her desperately, terrified.

Rosetta looks furious.

EXT. ABANDONED AIRFIELD - NIGHT

Hazel gently sets the broom down on the airstrip.
The Ghost staggers, then falls down and passes out.

Rosetta makes a steeper descent and a snazzier landing, whipping her broom out from under her and holding it up in front of her like a fighting staff.

Hazel stands in front of the Ghost, as if to defend him.
> ROSETTA
>That's one way to do an action scene.
>William Goldman, who wrote The Princess
>Bride, initiated that fragmented style
>to keep the one-minute-per-page ratio
>even when there isn't any dialogue to
>spread things out.

                    ROSETTA
        Lots of fragmented sentences and
        paragraph breaks.

Hazel looks at the corporeal Ghost with great
tenderness.

He is still passed out.

Hazel turns back to Rosetta and pouts, looking for
sympathy.

                    ROSETTA (CONT'D)
        Keep regular action-description
        short too. 3-4 lines per
        paragraph, max. Feature film
        writers don't get to talk about
        camera angles or shots, because
        it drives feature directors crazy
        (although TV writers do it all
        the time), so just describe
        briefly what the audience will
        see on screen. If you want to
        imply a new shot, start a new
        paragraph.

                    HAZEL
        Stop trying to distract me.

                    ROSETTA
        Who says I'm trying? You know
        he's no good.

EXT. MANOR HOUSE - NIGHT (FLASHBACK)

Hazel and Rosetta throw dirt into a shallow grave,
looking grimly satisfied.

                    ROSETTA (V.O.)
        That's why we killed him in the
        first place. Number your pages,
        starting with your second page,
        in the top right corner.

BACK TO SCENE:

EXT. ABANDONED AIRFIELD - NIGHT

Rosetta appeals to Hazel.

> ROSETTA
> BACK TO SCENE: or END FLASHBACK.
> both help to make the end of a
> flashback clearer.
>> (beat)
> Come on. Let me finish him off
> this time?

> HAZEL
> Maybe he's changed.

She steps aside to reveal his body, but --

He's gone.

Rosetta shoots Hazel an I-told-you-so look.

Hazel's phone RINGS.

> HAZEL (CONT'D)
> Hello?
>> (beat)
> Oh, hello. Where'd you go?
>> (flattered)
> You're welcome.

> ROSETTA
> Perfect. That's how you format a
> one-sided phone call.
>> (beat)
> If we wanna hear what he says
> too, we use (O.S.) and (filtered)
> for the dialogue of the person
> off screen.

> HAZEL
> Okay, okay.

> GHOST (O.S.)
>> (filtered)
> Are you letting Rosetta listen in?

                    HAZEL
          Yeah. So?

                    GHOST (O.S.)
                  (filtered)
          No, it's fine. But if you want
          the audience to see both people
          having a phone conversation, you
          need INTERCUT WITH: between
          scenes.

                    HAZEL
          Not you too.

                    ROSETTA
          He must have been there when you
          put the spell on me.

                                  INTERCUT WITH:

EXT. ABANDONED AIRFIELD PARKING — NIGHT

With the green VW Beetle behind him, the Ghost talks on
his cellphone in the parking lot.

Hazel talks into her phone on the airfield.

                    GHOST
          INTERCUT WITH: is useful when you
          want the director to film both
          sides of a phone conversation and
          the editor to cut back and forth
          between them. It's handy that you
          don't have to keep writing new
          scene headings once you've
          established both of them. You can
          skip (O.S.) and (filtered) too.
                  (then)
          My phone works again and I'm
          willing to bet my keys do too.

                    HAZEL
          What are you doing?

He opens the car and gets in, putting the phone on speaker in the cup holder. He opens the window so we still see him from outside.

> GHOST
> This car always was full of crap.

He pauses to throw a few things out of the open window: a lipstick, a handbag, a pair of sunglasses.

Hazel puffs across the airfield, still holding her broom.

The Ghost rolls his eyes and helps himself to a mint from the glove compartment, then starts the ENGINE.

Hazel starts to run toward the parking lot.

Rosetta gets onto her broom in a casual side-saddle pose and flies after her, just a few feet from the ground.

> HAZEL
> (panting)
> Hey? What's that noise? I'll be right there. Just wait for me. I thought you were going to haunt me?

He starts the ENGINE.

> GHOST
> That was only when I was ghostly and had nothing better to do.

He grins, ends the call, then drives off.

The last we see of him is a hand casually waving out of the open car window.

BEEP BEEP.

EXT. ABANDONED AIRFIELD - DAWN

Hazel stops running, then looks back at Rosetta gloomily.

Rosetta catches up.

> HAZEL
> Don't say I told you so.

> ROSETTA
> That scene heading said DAWN.
> Filmmakers prefer DAY or NIGHT,
> but writers occasionally write
> MORNING, AFTERNOON, SUNRISE,
> SUNSET, DAWN, or DUSK.
>   (beat)
> Sunrises and sunsets are
> expensive, so only use them as
> backdrops for your actors if you
> have a good story-based reason,
> like a vampire dying at dawn or
> an ex-con with a dusk curfew.

> HAZEL
>   (angry)
> Is there anything feature writers
> CAN'T put in a scene heading?

> ROSETTA
> CONTINUOUS, LATER, MOMENTS LATER,
> and SAME. TV writers use them,
> but it's best that feature
> writers don't, because feature
> filmmakers really do need to know
> whether it's DAY or NIGHT.
>   (beat)
> Did he take the car?

> HAZEL
> I don't want to talk about it.

Rosetta puts her arm around Hazel.

> ROSETTA
> Come on, let's fly back to your
> house before people start waking
> up and notice us.

They get onto their brooms.

INT. HAUNTED MANOR HOUSE DINING ROOM - DAY

Hazel walks slowly into the dining room. She sits down
at the table and starts filling two plates from all of
the cold dishes.

Hazel pours herself and Rosetta fresh glasses of wine.

                    ROSETTA (O.S.)
          Just washing my hands.

Rosetta enters and sits. They both cut their first bite
of the cold food.

                    ROSETTA (CONT'D)
          Just two more things, Hazel.

Hazel pauses, the bite on its way to her mouth.

                    ROSETTA (CONT'D)
          No scene numbers. We only add
          scene numbers to shooting scripts
          in pre-production.

                    HAZEL
          And the last thing?

                    ROSETTA
          Ah... structure.
               (beat)
          Feature scripts often have three
          acts (approx. 27, 55, and 25 pages).
          These aren't marked out on the page.
          You'll know an act break when you see
          one because either the protagonist
          embarks on a quest or there's a
          massive reversal. A short scene may
          show the new ordinary world after the
          climax.
               (beat)
          Thrillers often have five acts
          and action films have as many as
          seven (act one stays the same,
          then you divide up the rest).

Hazel puts down her fork.

> ROSETTA
> But feature-length TV movie of
> the week (M.O.W.) scripts — Xmas,
> mysteries, or thrillers — have act
> breaks marked on the pages. Capped,
> centered, and underlined. Like this:

END OF ACT ONE

ACT TWO

> ROSETTA
> A typical M.O.W. looks like this:
> ACT ONE — 25 pages
> ACT TWO — 13 pages
> ACT THREE — 10 pages
> ACT FOUR — 12 pages
> ACT FIVE — 10 pages
> ACT SIX — 10 pages
> ACT SEVEN — 10 pages
> ACT EIGHT — 10 pages
> TOTAL 110 pages
>
> The act breaks are commercial
> breaks, so they need cliffhangers.

> HAZEL
> (angry)
> Do you expect me to remember
> any of that?

> ROSETTA
> No. Sorry. I'll shut up now.

Hazel sits in front of the cold roast dinner, silently.

> HAZEL (V.O.)
> It was at that moment, that I
> started to plot my revenge.

FADE OUT.

THE END

MULTI-CAM SITCOM

Executive Producer: Kat Montagu
Executive Producer: Someone Fantastic

THE DREADED CURSE
SCREENPLAY FORMATTING
MULTI-CAM SITCOM

(Multi-Cam Sitcoms have logo-titles)
(For the pilot script, use bolded caps)

"Pilot"
(Episode title is lowercase
and in quotation marks)

Written by

Kat Montagu

(Revisions go on the right margin with a
color and the date, most recent draft first)

PINK REVISION PAGES 06/19/2X
BLUE REVISION PAGES 06/13/2X
SHOOTING DRAFT 06/12/2X
PRODUCTION DRAFT 06/02/2X
REVISED TABLE DRAFT 06/27/2X
TABLE DRAFT 05/20/2X
NETWORK DRAFT 04/03/2X

CAST LIST

HAZEL
ROSETTA
GHOST
DINER OWNER
YOGA BEAUTY
PORTUGUESE GRANDMA
COOK (VOICE ONLY)

<u>SET LIST</u>

INTERIORS

HAUNTED MANOR HOUSE DINING ROOM
LOS ANGELES MOTEL ROOM
LOS ANGELES DINER
VENICE BEACH BUNGALOW
   LIVING ROOM
   BATHROOM

EXTERIORS
LOS ANGELES MOTEL ROOM
VENICE CANAL BUNGALOW
LOS ANGELES DINER

COLD OPEN

INT. HAUNTED MANOR HOUSE DINING ROOM - NIGHT
(ROSETTA, HAZEL)

INTENSE <u>HAZEL</u> (24) AND HIPSTER <u>ROSETTA</u> (22) SIT WITH
THE MESSY REMAINS OF A MEAL.

> HAZEL
> So I'm clearly going to have to
>
> follow him to Los Angeles.

HAZEL PULLS HER LAPTOP OUT OF HER BAG AND STARTS
LOOKING FOR FLIGHTS. HER KEYBOARD <u>CLICKS</u>.

> ROSETTA
> How is <u>that</u> your take-away from
>
> this conversation? He was a
>
> terrible boyfriend. (BEAT) In
>
> multi-cam sitcoms, because
>
> action-descriptions are in caps,
>
> underlining makes <u>SOUNDS</u> or
>
> <u>EMPHASIS</u> or the first intro of a
>
> new character's <u>NAME</u> stand out.
>
> Good for dialogue emphasis too.

HAZEL IGNORES HER, TYPES RAPIDLY, THEN PRESSES ENTER.

> HAZEL
> Good. Two tickets, first thing
>
> tomorrow. Dibs on the window
>
> seat. Maybe we could take in a
>
> live sitcom taping?

                    ROSETTA
That sounds fun. Add a scene

header from p2 on. Click

Document, then Header and Footer.

                    HAZEL
Like the one at the top of this

page?

                    ROSETTA
Yes. They contain more info than

a feature header: **Series Title** in

bold, then "Episode Name" in

quotations, then numerical date,

then page number.

                    HAZEL
Hey! Why are we still talking

about screenplay formatting?

                    ROSETTA
I'm still under your spell to

teach you about formatting and we

haven't covered television yet.

                    HAZEL
You're kidding!

>   ROSETTA
> I wish I were. (BEAT) Multi-cam
>
> sitcom scripts don't need FADE
>
> IN: at the start. You do need to
>
> capitalize and underline scene
>
> headings, though.

ROSETTA FINISHES HER WINE.

>   HAZEL
> (GLOOMY) I still love him, you
>
> know.

>   ROSETTA
> What? Seriously? What is wrong
>
> with you? (HUFFS) Multi-cam
>
> sitcom parentheticals are most
>
> often on the same line as the
>
> dialogue in CAPITALS.

ROSETTA CROSSES TO FETCH A NEW BOTTLE OF WINE.

>   ROSETTA (CONT'D)
> The two of you were like TV
>
> sitcom characters: Sam and Diane,
>
> Rachel and Ross, Sheldon and Amy.

>   HAZEL
> All of those characters broke up.

>   ROSETTA
> Exactly!

> HAZEL
>
> Right, right. I know you're
>
> right.

> ROSETTA
>
> Multi-cam sitcom dialogue is
>
> double-spaced, which changes the
>
> ratio. For an episode that's 22
>
> minutes long -- a TV half-hour --
>
> the page count will be 44 pages
>
> or more. Some multi-cam sitcoms
>
> single space dialogue, but their
>
> scripts can still be 33 pages
>
> long.

HAZEL JUMPS UP.

> HAZEL
>
> That's it! We'd better pack.

> ROSETTA
>
> Okay, but please don't try to get
>
> him back.

> HAZEL
>
> (LYING) Of course not. I just
>
> want my car. I love that car.

> ROSETTA
>
> Right. I do too.

ROSETTA JUMPS UP TOO AND <u>CROSSES</u> TO THE DOOR.

>   ROSETTA (CONT'D)
> You have to write the act breaks
>
> where the commercial breaks go.
>
> These act breaks are capped,
>
> centered, underlined, and often
>
> also bolded. A typical sitcom has
>
> <u>**COLD OPEN**</u> (2-3 pages)
>
> <u>**ACT ONE**</u> (8-10 pages)
>
> <u>**ACT TWO**</u> (13-14 pages)
>
> <u>**ACT THREE**</u> (11-12 pages)
>
> <u>**TAG**</u> (1 page)
>
> But those page numbers can vary.
>
> (BEAT) Let's toast to our trip to
>
> Los Angeles... and to true love!

THEY <u>CLINK</u> THEIR GLASSES AND DRINK, THEN IT SINKS IN.

>   ROSETTA
> Wait! What?

OFF ROSETTA.

<u>**END OF COLD OPEN**</u>

ACT ONE

EXT. HOLLYWOOD SIGN — DAY

THE HOLLYWOOD SIGN. (STOCK FOOTAGE.)

EXT. LOS ANGELES MOTEL — DAY

The motel is classic LA, with a pool and palm trees.

INT. LOS ANGELES MOTEL ROOM — DAY
  (ROSETTA, HAZEL)

ROSETTA CHOOSES THE BED NEAR THE WINDOW, PUTS HER
SUITCASE ON IT, AND <u>CROSSES</u> TO ENTER THE BATHROOM.

HAZEL ENTERS.

> ROSETTA (O.C.)
> An off-screen character like
>
> myself is off-camera (O.C.). You
>
> probably noticed the Hollywood
>
> Sign and the Los Angeles Motel
>
> establishing shots before this
>
> scene and — way back at the
>
> start of this script — the list
>
> of locations immediately after
>
> the title page. Multi-cam sitcoms
>
> are filmed on standing sets with
>
> 5-8 locations, so they rarely
>
> shoot exteriors.

HAZEL SWAPS HER SUITCASE FOR ROSETTA'S, SITS DOWN, AND
LOOKS OUT OF THE WINDOW.

ROSETTA ENTERS.

                    ROSETTA
          Hey! I picked that bed.

HAZEL LIES DOWN ON IT, CHILDISHLY WRIGGLING.

                    HAZEL (CONT'D)
          What, this bed?

                    ROSETTA
          (SHRUGS) Single-spaced action-

          description (no more than four

          lines in a paragraph but usually

          less). Many multi-cam sitcom

          writers CAPITALIZE all of their

          action-description as I have

          here, but others don't.

HAZEL SITS ON THE OTHER BED.

                    HAZEL (CONT'D)
          Okay. Margins?

                    ROSETTA
          Same as a feature film script.

                    HAZEL
          (YAWNS) Okay, thanks. Good night.

HAZEL PUTS IN HER EARBUDS AND WATCHES TV ON HER PHONE.

ROSETTA ROLLS HER EYES.

Dreaded Curse   "Sitcom Pilot"   1/1/202X   8.

EXT. LOS ANGELES DINER - DAY

THE STREET IS BUSY. (STOCK FOOTAGE.)

INT. LOS ANGELES DINER — DAY
 (ROSETTA, HAZEL, DINER OWNER, YOGA BEAUTY, COOK)

Hazel drinks coffee and looks at a map on her phone.
A text from Rosetta: 'WHERE ARE YOU?'

Hazel texts back: 'DINER'

ROSETTA ENTERS AND SMILES AT THE HANDSOME DINER OWNER
(30) FOR COFFEE. HE IGNORES HER.

SHE'S ANNOYED AND TURNS TO HAZEL.

                    ROSETTA
          Have you noticed yet that the

          names of all the characters who

          will appear in a scene are capped

          in brackets beneath the scene

          heading with one space in front

          of them?

                    HAZEL
          Whatever! (LOOKS AT THE MAP) I

          think he's staying near here. He

          has a friend in the Venice Canal

          District.

                    ROSETTA
          Really? Near Venice Beach?

> HAZEL
> Yeah. She's a television writer.
>
> He's always wanted to write for
>
> television.

> ROSETTA
> Is she the one? You know? The
>
> other woman?

HAZEL SHRUGS.

THE HANDSOME DINER OWNER <u>CROSSES</u> WITH A <u>COFFEE POT</u> BUT
ONLY HAS EYES FOR HAZEL. HE POURS HER SOME COFFEE.

> DINER OWNER
> (TO HAZEL) Can I help you, miss?

> ROSETTTA
> Coffee, please?

> DINER OWNER
> (TO HAZEL) How about something
>
> for breakfast?

> ROSETTA
> Thanks. Just the coffee for now.

DINER OWNER WALKS AWAY WITHOUT GIVING ROSETTA COFFEE.

> ROSETTA
> Wait! (TURNS TO HAZEL) What's
>
> wrong with him?

HAZEL DRINKS HER COFFEE WITH RELISH.

> HAZEL
> Don't know. He makes great
>
> coffee, though.

>   ROSETTA
>   (CALLS) Hello. Coffee, please?

DINER OWNER IGNORES HER AND CHATS TO <u>YOGA BEAUTY</u> (30).

>   YOGA BEAUTY
>   Egg white omelet, to go please?

>   DINER OWNER
>   Coming right up.

HE JOTS IT DOWN ON HIS <u>PAD</u>, RIPS OFF THE PAGE, PUSHES
IT THROUGH THE PASS-THROUGH, AND GIVES YOGA BEAUTY
COFFEE.

>   ROSETTA
>   <u>UNDERLINE AND CAPITALIZE</u> each new
>
>   character the first time you
>
>   introduce them in action. (BEAT)
>
>   May I have a sip of your coffee?

>   HAZEL
>   Why don't we just order
>
>   breakfast, then you can have your
>
>   own? (CALLS OVER TO DINER OWNER)
>
>   Two specials please, and two
>
>   coffees.

DINER OWNER NODS, SCRIBBLES DOWN THE ORDER, COMES OVER
WITH HIS <u>COFFEE POT</u>, AND FILLS THEM BOTH UP.

>   ROSETTA
>   (UNGRATEFUL) Thanks.

>   DINER OWNER
>   (TO HAZEL) You're welcome.

WITH A RAISED BROW, THE DINER OWNER WALKS AWAY.

                    ROSETTA
          When you're around, I might as

          well be invisible.

HAZEL SHRUGS APOLOGETICALLY.

THE YOGA BEAUTY STRETCHES -- SUPER-FLEXIBLE -- BUT THE
DINER OWNER STILL LOOKS AT HAZEL.

                    COOK (O.C.)
          Egg white omelet to go.

THE DINER OWNER HANDS YOGA BEAUTY THE FOOD. SHE EXITS.

EXT. VENICE CANAL BUNGALOW — NIGHT
  (HAZEL, ROSETTA, PORTUGUESE GRANDMA)

HAZEL GLANCES AROUND, CONSULTING HER PHONE.

                    HAZEL
          I think this is the one.

                    ROSETTA
          That's what you said about the

          last four houses.

HAZEL KNOCKS. A PORTUGUESE GRANDMA (75) EMERGES FROM
THE BUNGALOW CARRYING A SHOPPING BASKET.

                    PORTUGUESE GRANDMA
          (HOW CAN I HELP YOU?) Como posso

          ajudá-lo?

                    HAZEL
          (TO ROSETTA) Have I forgotten how

          to speak Spanish?

                    ROSETTA
          That's Portuguese. (BEAT) As well

          as using parentheticals for tone

          or small pieces of action while

          talking, in a sitcom script you

          can use them to direct a line to

          a specific person or to

          translate.

Rosetta smiles at the Portuguese Grandma.

                    ROSETTA (CONT'D)
          (WE'RE LOOKING FOR A HANDSOME

          GHOSTLY MAN?) Umm ... Estamos

          procurando por um belo homem ...

          fantasmagórico?

                    PORTUGUESE GRANDMA
          I speak English. He's out. You

          can wait inside, if you like.

                    HAZEL
          Yes, please.

PORTUGUESE GRANDMA WHIPS OUT HER CELLPHONE, AND TAKES
THEIR PHOTO.

                    PORTUGUESE GRANDMA
          In case you steal something!

THE PORTUGUESE GRANDMA CROSSES AND LEAVES.

                    ROSETTA
          How rude!

HAZEL AND ROSETTA ENTER.

<u>INT. BUNGALOW LIVING ROOM — CONTINUOUS</u>
  (ROSETTA, HAZEL, GHOST)

THE BUNGALOW IS BRIGHT AND HAS VIEWS OF THE CANAL.

                    ROSETTA
          Did you notice that it says

          CONTINUOUS in that scene heading?

          Once TV writers establish whether

          it's DAY or NIGHT, they often use

          CONTINUOUS, LATER, MOMENTS LATER,

          or SAME for subsequent scenes.

                    HAZEL
          I did notice that. But you hate

          it so much in features.

                    ROSETTA
          When in Burbank, do what the

          Burbankians do.

                    HAZEL
          Is it Burbankians or Burbankers?

                    ROSETTA
          No idea. Let's face it, every

          television sitcom series is

          formatted a little bit

          differently.

ROSETTA SHOWS HAZEL HER CELLPHONE.

> ROSETTA
> Why not read some recent
>
> teleplays online?

THE GHOST (26) MAKES A SUDDEN AND DRAMATIC ENTRANCE,
DRESSED NOW IN COOL LOS ANGELES CLOTHES AND AVIATORS.

> GHOST
> Can I help you... ladies?

> HAZEL
> What? It's me, Hazel. My hair's
>
> grown a bit but surely...

HE SHRUGS.

> ROSETTA
> (TOUGH) We want the car back.

> GHOST
> (TO ROSETTA) Too late. I sold it.

HE POPS HIS CUFFS TO REVEAL A FANCY WATCH.
WHEN THE GIRLS STARE BLANKLY, HE LOOKS ANNOYED.

> GHOST
> You know, like George Clooney's.

> HAZEL
> You mean, you sold my car to buy
>
> a watch like George Clooney's?

> GHOST
> Gotta look like a Burbanker.

HAZEL NUDGES ROSETTA.

                    HAZEL
See! Burbanker!

                    ROSETTA
(TO HAZEL) Whatever. He's like a

walking courtroom TV episode.

Let's call the police.

                    HAZEL
(TO ROSETTA) And tell them what?

That Ghost stole my car?

                    ROSETTA
I'm willing to bet he couldn't

break out of a jail cell anymore.

ROSETTA PINCHES THE GHOST.

                    ROSETTA
Feels pretty solid to me.

                    GHOST
(FLIRTY) Thanks.

                    ROSETTA
It wasn't a compliment, you

idiot.

HE POUTS AND FLEXES HIS BICEPS.

                    GHOST
Oh no? Check out this gun show.

ROSETTA ROLLS HER EYES.

                    GHOST
          (TO ROSETTA) Maybe I was

     romancing the wrong sister?

                    HAZEL
          Hey! Why are you paying so much

     attention to her?

                    GHOST
          (FINALLY TURNS TO HAZEL) Ha! I

     know what you did to me, you

     witch!

ROSETTA ZAPS HIM WITH HER WAND, FREEZING HIM WHERE HE
STANDS. ONLY HIS EYES CAN MOVE.

                    ROSETTA
          What's he talking about?

                    HAZEL
          Who knows!

ROSETTA ACCEPTS THIS. ROSETTA TAKES THE <u>WATCH</u> OFF HIS
WRIST, PULLS HIS <u>WALLET</u> OUT (WITH A GROSS EXPRESSION,
AS SHE ACCIDENTALLY TOUCHES HIS BUTT), AND FINDS THE
<u>RECEIPT</u> FOR THE WATCH.

                    ROSETTA
          We're going to return this and

     buy back your car.

                    HAZEL
               (looks at Ghost)
          We can't just leave him like

     this.

ROSETTA ASSESSES HIM, PLACES HIS HANDS IN A CHEESY TWO THUMBS UP, PULLS HIS PANTS DOWN TO REVEAL <u>RED SPEEDOS</u>, AND ASSESSES HIM AGAIN.

> ROSETTA
> Better.

ROSETTA EXITS.

HAZEL FOLLOWS HER OUT.

> HAZEL (O.C.)
> Tell me that's gonna wear off.

> ROSETTA (O.C.)
> Sure it will -- the moment

Grandma gets home.

ONLY GHOST'S EYES MOVE AS HE LOOKS DOWN DESPERATELY.

<u>EXT. VENICE BEACH BUNGALOW — DAY</u>

HAZEL AND ROSETTA HIDE BEHIND A SHRUB AND WATCH THROUGH THE WINDOW AS —

<u>INT. VENICE BEACH BUNGALOW — DAY</u>

PORTUGUESE GRANDMA ENTERS.

> PORTUGUESE GRANDMA
> (HOLY SHIT!) Puta que pariu!

GHOST UNFREEZES FROM HIS EMBARRASSING FONZIE POSE.

PORTUGUESE GRANDMA CHASES HIM OUT OF THE BUNGALOW WITH THE BROOM AS HE TRIES IN VAIN TO PULL HIS PANTS UP, THEN TRIPS OVER THEM.

WE CAN SEE AND HEAR HAZEL AND ROSETTA <u>LAUGHING</u>.

<u>END OF SHOW</u>

SINGLE-CAM HALF-HOUR

Executive Producer: Kat Montagu
Executive Producer: Someone Fantastic

THE DREADED CURSE
SCREENPLAY FORMATTING
SINGLE-CAM HALF-HOUR

(Single-Cam Half-Hour shows have logo-titles)
(For the pilot script, use bolded caps)

"Pilot"
or
EP #118: "Fun Time"

Written by

Kat Montagu

Directed by

Someone Fabulous

(Revisions go on the right
margin with color and date)
BLUE REVISION PAGES 06/13/2X
PINK REVISION PAGES 06/18/2X
YELLOW REVISION PAGES 06/19/2X

PROD. #: 1ATM2X
STORY #: E06784

<u>**DREADED CURSE**</u>

<u>EPISODE #101</u>

Many single-cam half-hour shows don't have cast lists or set lists, but if you do plan to add them, this is how.

<u>CAST LIST</u>

```
HAZEL.........................................Name of Actor
ROSETTA.......................................Name of Actor
GHOST.........................................Name of Actor
DINER OWNER...................................Name of Actor
YOGA BEAUTY...................................Name of Actor
PORTUGUESE GRANDMA............................Name of Actor
HEMSWORTH.....................................Name of Actor
OLD LADY......................................Name of Actor
```

DREADED CURSE

EPISODE #101

SET LIST

Here are two ways of formatting the set list for a single-cam half-hour show:

1)
INTERIORS

LOS ANGELES MOTEL ROOM

LOS ANGELES DINER

VENICE BEACH BUNGALOW
*LIVING ROOM
*BATHROOM

EXTERIORS
VENICE BOARDWALK PARKING

VENICE BEACH

LOS ANGELES DINER

2)

INTERIORS	EXTERIORS
LOS ANGELES MOTEL ROOM	VENICE BOARDWALK PARKING
LOS ANGELES DINER	VENICE BEACH
VENICE BEACH BUNGALOW - LIVING ROOM - BATHROOM	LOS ANGELES DINER

COLD OPEN

EXT. LOS ANGELES DINER - DAY

HAZEL, 24, tightly-wound in a floaty black dress with
new highlights, and ROSETTA, 22, a relaxed hipster in
an activist tee, arrive at the diner in Hazel's beloved
GREEN VW BEETLE.

Rosetta pats the dashboard.

                    HAZEL
      I can't believe we got my car back.

Rosetta takes a large gulp from her water bottle.

                  HAZEL (CON'D)
      Wait! Isn't that a Hemsworth?

Rosetta turns to look as --

HEMSWORTH walks by in the golden glow of stardom.

Rosetta spit-takes right into the crotch of Hemsworth's
linen pants. Looks like he wet himself.

Rosetta's so embarrassed.

                    HAZEL
      Wait. That was a classic spit-take and
      nobody laughed!

                  ROSETTA
      Single-camera half-hour shows aren't
      filmed in front of a live audience,
      and they don't have laugh tracks.

                  HAZEL
    Oh.

Hemsworth looks furious, but ignores Rosetta, notices
Hazel, and winks at her.

                  ROSETTA
    What the hell!

But it's too late, they turn the corner.

Dreaded Curse - #203 - Yellow Rev. Draft - 10/13/2X   2.

Hemsworth shrugs and adjusts his wet crotch, just as --

AN OLD LADY (70s) walks by and looks disapprovingly.

Hemsworth winks at her too.

She preens.

EXT. VENICE BOARDWALK PARKING - DAY

The green VW Beetle zooms up.

                    ROSETTA
          Cute guys never notice me anymore.
          Have I lost my mojo?

                    HAZEL
               (shrugs and avoids her eyes)
          How come we're shooting in exterior
          locations?

                    ROSETTA
          Single-cam half-hour series often use
          real-world filming locations.
               (looks back)
          That was my only chance to meet a
          Hemsworth and he didn't even see me...
          even though I spit water on him.

                    HAZEL
          Oh, Rosetta. All that really matters
          is revenge.

                    ROSETTA
          What? No! Now we have the car back,
          let's take a vacation.

                    HAZEL
          A vacation? Really?

Rosetta shrugs.

                    HAZEL (CONT'D)
          He broke my heart. For that, he must
          suffer.

                    ROSETTA
We embarrassed him. Isn't that enough?
      (beat)
I'm not sure he's capable of real
suffering, anyway.

                    HAZEL
I can fix that... Maybe.
      (distracted)
Wait a second. I thought this was
supposed to be a half-hour show. Why
isn't it funnier?

                    ROSETTA
Single-camera shows can be comedy-
dramas.

                    HAZEL
Well, it's pretty light on the comedy.
To be totally honest, I prefer a one-
hour dramatic format.

                    ROSETTA
I can do something about that. Before
we go, remember that because dialogue
in a single-cam half-hour show is
single-spaced, the ratio's different.
So 32 to 37 pages for a 22 minute
episode. A typical episode structure:
      (beat)
COLD OPEN (4 pages)
ACT ONE (9 pages)
ACT TWO (6-9 pages)
ACT THREE (7-9 pages)
Single-cam scripts either end with:
ACT FOUR (2-5 pages)
or with a **TAG** (1 page)

SMASH TO TITLES:
DREADED CURSE

                    END OF COLD OPEN

One-Hour Drama

EXEC. PRODUCER: NAME
EXEC. PRODUCER: NAME
CO-EXEC. PRODUCER: NAME
CO-EXEC. PRODUCER: NAME
PRODUCED BY: NAME
PRODUCER: NAME
CO-PRODUCER: NAME

THE DREADED CURSE
SCREENPLAY FORMATTING
ONE-HOUR DRAMA
(logo later)

"Pilot"

Story by
Kat Montagu

Screenplay by
Kat Montagu

REVISED WRITERS DRAFT - 5/30/2X
WHITE PRODUCTION DRAFT - 5/30/2X
BLUE DRAFT - 6/07/2X
PINK DRAFT - 6/12/2X
YELLOW DRAFT - 6/14/2X
GREEN DRAFT - 6/17/2X
GOLDENROD DRAFT - 6/24/2X
BUFF DRAFT - 6/30/2X
SALMON DRAFT - 7/01/2X
CHERRY DRAFT - 7/07/2X
TAN DRAFT - 7/14/2X
2nd BLUE DRAFT - 7/29/2X
2nd PINK DRAFT - 7/30/2X

(Note: Some productions include revised page numbers too.
Like this: 5/30/2X - White Prod. Draft - pgs. 16-36)

THE DREADED CURSE

"Pilot"

<u>CAST LIST</u>

HAZEL
ROSETTA
GHOST

DINER OWNER

CHUNKY COP
CHATTY COP

(Separate cast into bunches:

Series regulars

Recurring characters

Episodic characters)

THE DREADED CURSE

"Pilot"

SET LIST

INTERIORS:

HAUNTED MANOR HOUSE
- DINING ROOM

LOS ANGELES MOTEL ROOM

LOS ANGELES DINER

VENICE BEACH BUNGALOW
- LIVING ROOM
- BATHROOM

EXTERIORS:

LOS ANGELES MOTEL

VENICE CANAL BUNGALOW

LOS ANGELES DINER

VENICE BEACH STREET

(There are many subtly different ways to arrange title pages, draft revisions, cast lists, and set lists. One important thing to remember is that most TV writers are also producers, so by choosing the number of characters and the number of locations, you're controlling the budget.)

(Many TV writers know how many guest stars per episode and how many Interior and Exterior shots they can afford. A large-budget superhero show might have 20 interiors mostly reused over multiple episodes and 15 exteriors in a single episode. A lower-budget dramatic show might have 8 interiors and 15 exteriors.)

DREADED CURSE "Pilot" - 8/01/2X   (2ND YELLOW DRAFT)   1.

                              TEASER

     FADE IN:

1.   EXT. VENICE BEACH STREET — DAY   1.

     HAZEL and ROSETTA walk along the sidewalk, both
     wearing cute Los Angeles outfits. Hazel has
     California highlights in her hair.

                         HAZEL
               There's a header on this first page.

                         ROSETTA
               Some one-hour drama writers do that.
               Others start them on the second page.
                    (beat)
               Hey, what are we doing here?

                         HAZEL
               We're here for revenge, remember?

                         ROSETTA
               Right, but we already got the car
               back, and it's not worth much, anyway.
               There was one online for two grand.

                         HAZEL
               It's not about the car.

     Camera tilts up to find a palm tree.

                         HAZEL (O.C.)
               I thought we weren't allowed to
               mention cameras or shots?

     On Hazel and Rosetta again.

                         ROSETTA
               In TV scripts we are, especially one-
               hour dramas. Remember the showrunner
               (credited as the Executive Producer)
               is also the head writer.

                                        (CONTINUED)

DREADED CURSE "Pilot" - 8/01/2X   (2ND YELLOW DRAFT)   2.

1.   CONTINUED: (2)   1.

                    HAZEL
          Hey! What's the deal with those
          continueds?

                    ROSETTA
          TV writers often use them to show that
          the scene goes onto the next page. The
          (2) shows how many pages there have
          been in this scene so far.
                    (beat)
          Right. Look, there he is!

On a bench across the street sits the Ghost.

Just as Hazel and Rosetta move to cross the road and
confront him, a police car arrives, SIRENS BLARING.

2.   EXT. BENCH — CONTINUOUS   2.

CHUNKY COP (40) and his partner CHATTY COP (23) leap
out of their squad car. They confront the Ghost.
Chunky Cop cuffs him.

                    CHUNKY COP
          You have the right to remain silent.
          Anything you say can and will be used
          against you in a court of law. You
          have the right to an attorney...

                    GHOST
          But what are you arresting me for?

                    CHATTY COP
          The murder of an innocent grandmother.

                    CHUNKY COP
          Shush! We're the ones asking
          questions.

                    GHOST
          But she was alive when I saw her this
          morning.

                                        (CONTINUED)

DREADED CURSE "Pilot" - 8/01/2X   (2ND YELLOW DRAFT)   3.

2.   CONTINUED: (2)   2.

Chunky Cop puts his hand on the Ghost's head and ducks
him into the back seat of the police car.

3.   EXT. VENICE BEACH STREET — CONTINUOUS   3.

Across the street, Hazel glances at Rosetta.

                    ROSETTA
          We're not helping him. Revenge,
          remember --

                    HAZEL
          Hey! I didn't interrupt you. Shouldn't
          that be an ellipsis?

                    ROSETTA
          Television writers use double dashes
          all the time, for fragmented
          sentences, or instead of periods at
          the end of sentences, usually with a
          leading space --

                    HAZEL
               (thinks)
          Look, you can do what you want, but I
          have to help him --

                    ROSETTA
               (gives up)
          Alright. Where do we start?

                    HAZEL
          Let's start with you showing me a
          superhero show action paragraph.

Hazel races down the CROWDED street -- dragging her
SISTER with her -- COLLIDING with PEDESTRIANS --

                                        (CONTINUED)

3.   CONTINUED: (2)   3.

                         ROSETTA
            Hold on!

Rosetta trips over someone's large RUNNING SHOE -- and
SPRAWLS on the sidewalk --

Hazel reluctantly stops and turns --

The Diner Owner ignores Rosetta and addresses Hazel.

                         DINER OWNER
                    (to Hazel)
            Hey, it's you again. Your hair looks
            nice. What's going on?

Hazel helps Rosetta up.

                         ROSETTA
            Hazel's ex just got arrested for
            murder!

                         DINER OWNER
                    (to Hazel)
            I'm so sorry. What can I do to help?

                         HAZEL
            We should probably go and bail him
            out. Do you have any money?

                         DINER OWNER
                    (to Hazel)
            Sure. There's an ATM on the next
            corner.

                         ROSETTA
                    (to the Diner Owner)
            Excuse us for just a second.

The Diner Owner doesn't look at Rosetta.

                                              (CONTINUED)

DREADED CURSE "Pilot" - 8/01/2X   (2ND YELLOW DRAFT)   5.

3.   CONTINUED: (3)   3.

                          HAZEL
           We just need a moment.

                          DINER OWNER
           Sure thing.

     They take a few steps away from him. While they talk,
     he waits, patiently.

                          ROSETTA
                     (whispers)
           Why is a total stranger offering to
           bail out your ex-boyfriend, Hazel?
           What have you done?

                      END OF ACT ONE

                         ACT TWO

4.   EXT. VENICE BEACH STREET — DAY   4.

     Rosetta looks furious.

                          HAZEL
                     (reluctant whisper)
           I might have done a teeny-tiny spell.

     A CUTE GUY (24) walks past them -- WINKS at Hazel and
     completely ignores Rosetta.

                          ROSETTA
           Is that why men ignore me when you're
           around?

                          HAZEL
           Why do you always have to be the
           center of attention? Hey, tell me
           about how to format a one-hour
           television episode!

                                            (CONTINUED)

4.   CONTINUED: (2)   4.

                    ROSETTA
          Okay. One-Hour Television Episode:
          <u>TEASER</u> — 2 pages (some skip teasers)
          <u>ACT ONE</u> — 8-13 pages
          <u>ACT TWO</u> — 9-12 pages
          <u>ACT THREE</u> — 10-13 pages
          <u>ACT FOUR</u> — 8-13 pages
          <u>ACT FIVE</u> — 6-13 pages
          <u>ACT SIX</u> — 10-14 pages
          Some writers skip Act Six and instead:
          <u>TAG/STING</u> — 1 page
          Total 55-65 pages
          You'll need a cliffhanger at the end
          of each of these acts.

                    HAZEL
          What about Video On Demand streamers?

                    ROSETTA
          Many VOD shows don't have act breaks
          written in unless they're also airing
          on a terrestrial network, but they
          still have inherent unwritten act
          breaks like feature scripts.

     Rosetta shakes her head.

                    ROSETTA (CONT'D)
               (loud now)
          Hey!!! You're manipulating me using
          magic. Is this what you did to your
          ex?

                                        (CONTINUED)

4.   CONTINUED: (3)   4.

                        HAZEL
                   (pouts)
              He wasn't paying enough attention
              to me.

                        ROSETTA
              Did he even cheat on you, the way
              you said?

                        HAZEL
                   (lying)
              Maybe.

                        ROSETTA
              You're the worst!

Rosetta pulls out her wand and points it at Hazel.

                        ROSETTA (CONT'D)
              Undo.

A spark emits from the end of Rosetta's wand -- it
circles Hazel and undoes every trace of magic.

Immediately, Hazel's cute Los Angeles outfit turns
back into her original black dress. The highlights
vanish from her hair.

A few feet away, the Diner Owner shakes his head in
disbelief and exits.

                        HAZEL
              Great. Now what'll I do?

                        ROSETTA
              You'll bail him out yourself, then you
              and I will figure out who really
              killed that sweet old grandma and
              bring them to justice.

                                              (CONTINUED)

DREADED CURSE "Pilot" - 8/01/2X   (2ND YELLOW DRAFT)   8.

4.   CONTINUED: (4)   4.

Hazel looks very grumpy. They head back to the car.

>   HAZEL
> Aren't you going to tell me how to end
> a one-hour television script?

>   ROSETTA
> No! You can figure it out for
> yourself!

>   HAZEL
> Really?

Rosetta stomps ahead.

Hazel discreetly pulls her wand out of her bag, and
mouths these words MOS (without sound).

>   HAZEL
>   (silently)
> Remember, remember, the 5th of--

Rosetta turns and catches her.

>   ROSETTA
> Hazel!

Hazel smiles guiltily, busted.

<u>END OF SHOW</u>

Index

(use grey page numbers for navigation)

About the Author

Kat Montagu is a writer, a story editor, and a full-time screenwriting instructor at Vancouver Film School. She has a BFA and an MFA in Creative Writing and has also taught at the University of British Columbia and Emily Carr University of Art & Design.

Born in the UK, Kat lives in Vancouver, Canada with her husband Rob Wenzek, their daughter Lydia, and their terriers Astro and Oscar.

CPSIA information can be obtained
at www.ICGtesting.com
Printed in the USA
LVHW010345050821
694541LV00011B/1157

9 781988 915333